CURIOUS
Questions & answers about...
My Body

How TALL are you?

If you could have one super power for a day, what would it be?

What's your favourite way to keep fit?

Do you prefer sweet or savoury food?

If you could have an extra sense, what would it be?

Do you go to bed early or late?

Words by Anne Rooney

Illustrations by Ana Gomez

MILES KELLY

What is my body for?

Your body lets you see, hear, smell, taste and touch the world around you. You can use it to run, jump, think, talk, and have all kinds of fun. Without it, you couldn't do anything.

> Our bodies look different on the outside, but inside we all have bones, muscles and blood.

> Cells make up tissue such as bone, muscle and blood.

Why are cells so special?

Because they are the tiny building blocks that together make up your body. Different cells do different jobs. You have blood cells, bone cells, skin cells and lots more.

Bone cells make up your skeleton

X-rays can check for broken bones.

How can doctors see inside our bodies?

Doctors can look inside the body with scans and X-rays to see where all the parts are and how they fit together. They can even look at single cells with microscopes that magnify them.

Muscle cells help to form every muscle in your body

Your blood contains trillions of red blood cells

Why do I need to eat?

Food provides the energy your body needs to keep working. Chemicals from food repair your body and help it grow. Your body breaks down food and rearranges the chemicals to make skin, hair, bones and all the other parts.

Can I balance my food?

Yes you can, but not on your head! It's important to eat a wide range of foods from different food groups to make sure you stay fit and healthy.

Fruit and vegetables
Eat lots of these for fibre and goodness

Protein
Meat, fish and beans help your body grow and repair itself

Sugar and fats give you energy, but eating too much of them can be unhealthy.

Fats and sugars
Foods high in fats and sugars should only be eaten in small amounts

Carbohydrates
Bread, potatoes, rice and pasta give you lots of energy

Dairy
Milk, cheese and yoghurt keep your bones and teeth strong

Drink lots of water!

Eat five portions of fruit and vegetables every day.

Why is water so important?

About 60 percent of your body is water – it's in every cell. But you lose water when you pee and sweat, and every time you breathe out. You need to drink to replace the water you lose.

What happens when I eat?

The food you eat takes a long and twisty route through your digestive system. At each stage, your body pulls out the good things it needs.

Always wash your hands before eating.

① How do teeth help?

Your teeth break up food as you chew. They chew it into smaller pieces and mash it around. Food mixes with saliva in your mouth, making it easier to swallow.

② Where does food go first?

When you swallow, food goes into a tube in your throat called your oesophagus (say 'ee-sof-a-guss'). Muscles push the food down to your stomach, squeezing behind the lump of food so that it moves along.

Oesophagus

From mouth to stomach takes 5–8 seconds

③ Why is there acid in my stomach?

Acid dissolves food into a gloopy liquid. Muscles in your stomach also churn the mixture around to break it up.

④ What goes on in my intestines?

A milky mushy liquid moves into and through your intestines where nutrients (useful chemicals) and water are absorbed. The leftover parts are turned into... poo!

⑤ Why do I need to poo?

To get rid of the bits that your body doesn't need. These parts are squashed together and mixed with dead cells and water from your gut. They leave your body when you go to the toilet.

Always wash your hands after going to the toilet.

We're going down! Weee!

Food stays in your stomach for 2–6 hours. It turns to a milky mush called chyme (say 'kime')

Stomach GLOOP!

③

④ Large intestine

Small intestine

POO!

⑤

The journey through your intestines can take 12–18 hours

How many?

35 The number of tonnes of food the average person eats in their life.

110,000 The number of hairs on the head of a dark-haired person; blondes have more and redheads have fewer.

37 trillion The number of human cells in an adult body.

1.5–2 The area in square metres of an adult's skin.

0.5 The volume of gas in litres that your gut produces each day.

Your nose can detect **1 trillion** smells.

69 The largest number of babies anyone has had.

16
The speed in kilometres per hour of a sneeze.

A hair grows **1.25** centimetres each month.

900
The length in centimetres of the longest-ever fingernail.

120
The speed in metres per second of a message travelling along a nerve.

5
The amount in litres of blood in an average adult human.

3
The length in millimetres of your smallest bone (it's inside your ear).

What is my skeleton made of?

Bones form the rigid framework for your body – your skeleton. They support your body and provide somewhere for your muscles to fix to.

Imagine how floppy and blobby you'd be without bones!

Skull

Clavic[le]

Jaw

Humerus

Ribs

Sternum

Ulna

Spine

Radius

Pelvis

Femur

Patella

Fibula

Tibia

Phalanges

How do muscles move me?

Most muscles are fixed to your bones. As they contract, they pull the bones along with them, moving your body. Being active makes your muscles strong. Run, swim, jump, cycle – do anything you like!

Biceps muscle contracts to bend your arm

contract

relax

Tendon attaches muscle to bone

Triceps muscle relaxes

Which muscle works the hardest?

Your heart works harder than any other muscle. It never stops pumping blood around your body throughout your life.

How does my body bend?

You have lots of joints in your body such as in your knees, elbows, shoulders, ankles and wrists. These are places where bones meet, and they allow your body to bend or move in different ways.

Activities like swimming make you breathe fast

Lung

Heart

Lung

What happens when I breathe?

When you breathe in, your lungs fill with air. Oxygen from the air goes into your blood and is delivered to your whole body. Old air is pushed out when you breathe out.

How does my blood deliver oxygen?

Your blood flows through tubes called blood vessels. These reach every single part of your body to make sure you have all the oxygen you need. Your heart and blood together are called the circulatory system.

Blood vessels

Why does my heart thump?

When you exercise, your heart beats faster to pump blood around your body quickly, to deliver the oxygen your muscles need. You also breathe faster to get more oxygen, and you feel out of breath.

Why can't I breathe underwater?

Because you don't have gills like a fish! Your lungs can only take oxygen from the air. A fish's gills can take dissolved oxygen from water. When you swim underwater, you need to come to the surface for air.

Why am I ticklish?

Because you have a sense of touch! Your body uses five senses to find out about the world around you. Your senses pick up information and send it to your brain.

Smell — Cells in your nose help you recognize smells

See — Eyes let in light to help you see all around you

Hear — Ears pick up sound vibrations to help you hear

Taste — Special areas on your tongue tell you what something tastes like

Touch — Skin is packed with touch sensors to help you feel

Why can't I see in the dark?

Because you need light to bounce off objects and into your eyes. A lens in your eye helps focus the light, and a nerve carries information to your brain to make an image — and that is what you see.

Lens

Optic nerve to brain

Why are ears a funny shape?

The shape of your ears helps to funnel sound into them. Sound is then carried inside your ear, where signals are sent along a nerve to your brain, so it can make sense of what you hear.

The outer ear is called the pinna

Soundwaves in

Tiny ear bones

Auditory nerve to brain

How do I smell?

Your sense of smell is produced by cells high above and behind your nose. Tiny particles of the thing you are smelling reach those cells.

Tiny cells detect smell particles and send signals to your brain

Smell particles go up your nose

What helps me taste food?

Your tongue is covered with blobs surrounded by tiny taste buds. The taste buds send messages to your brain about the chemicals dissolved in food, and your brain turns the information into tastes.

Did you know?

Your **teeth** are as strong as a **shark's** teeth – but your jaws are smaller so you can't bite like a shark.

Babies can hear before they're born, though sounds from the outside are a bit **muffled**.

I hope I grow up to be a better singer than Mum.

An **adult** can survive three weeks without **food**, but only about four days without **water**.

Your **ears** are important to your sense of **balance**.

In **complete darkness,** your eyes could spot the light from a candle 48 kilometres away.

Some parts of your body are never replaced. The **enamel** on your teeth and the **goo** inside your **eyes** have to last a lifetime.

By the time you were six months old, your **eyes** were already **two thirds** their adult size.

Children can hear higher sounds than adults, including **bats** squeaking and **ultrasonic** dog whistles.

Fingerprints are not the body's only unique pattern. You can also be identified by your **tongue print**, your personal **smell** and the pattern in your **iris** (the coloured part of your eye).

Your **blood** is made inside your **bones.**

Is my brain in charge?

What you say, think and how you move, and everything else you do, is controlled by your brain.

It receives information

A network of nerves tells your brain what is happening to your body. Your brain is linked to your body by your spinal cord

Brain

Spinal cord

Stand on one foot and spin the ball.

It sends messages

Your brain sends messages to your body, telling it how to react or move

Nerve network

Nerve cell

What do my nerves do?

Nerves are collections of nerve cells (neurons). They carry information between all parts of your body and brain. When you see, smell, taste or hear anything, information is carried by nerves to your brain super-quickly.

5

Your brain is protected by your skull, and a layer of fluid

Think and plan

Touch and taste

Talk and smell

Hear

See

Move

Different areas of your brain control different things

How do I remember things?

Everything is stored in your brain, including memories, dreams and what you've learnt at school. Your brain stores some information for just seconds, and some for a lifetime.

④

Why do we say 'ouch'?

If you touch something hot, nerves carry signals to your spinal cord (1). This responds immediately (2) and sends a message through other nerves to make your hand move away (3). A slower message goes to your brain (4) that makes you feel pain and say 'ouch'.

Spinal cord

①

②

③

Why do I sleep?

Your body uses the time you're asleep to repair any injuries, grow, rest and sort out what you've experienced and learnt during the day. No one knows exactly how sleep works, but we do know that we can't live without it.

Does everyone dream?

Yes, but not everyone remembers their dreams. Most people have 3-5 dreams each night. Even cats and dogs have dreams!

No one knows what animals dream about!

Why are dreams so weird?

As your brain sorts through information while you sleep, it's in a jumbled order, with recent events mixed up with old memories. Some people think secret meanings are hidden in dreams.

Each dream can last 20 minutes or a few seconds

How much sleep do I need?

We need different amounts of sleep at different ages. Newborn babies sleep for a long time every day. Adults sleep less.

Hours

18
16
14
12
10
8
6
4
2
0

Newborn Pre-school School Teen Adult

23

Would you rather?

Be able to breathe underwater or be **light** enough to walk on top of the water?

Have a really long **tongue** or really long **fingers**?

Have **super-keen sight** or be able to hear very **quiet sounds** like ants munching their food?

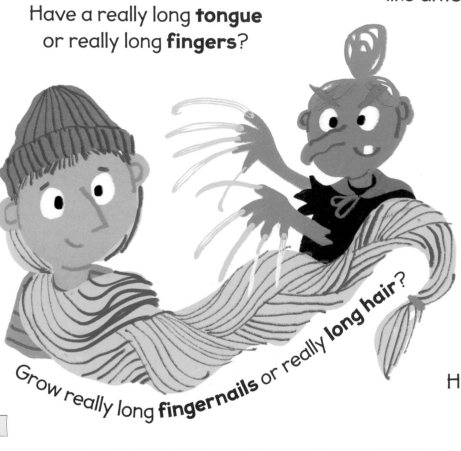

Grow really long **fingernails** or really **long hair**?

Have **unbreakable** bones or **uncuttable** skin?

Have **wings** or a **tail**?

Be **wobbly** like a jellyfish with no bones, or have a **hard** outer shell like a tortoise?

Be entirely **furry** or entirely **bald**?

Have eyes in the back of your **head** or in the tips of your **fingers**?

Be able to run really **fast** or for a really **long** time?

25

Where do babies come from?

Babies come from inside their mum's body. A baby grows in the mum's uterus, where it gets everything it needs until it's ready to be born.

Cord

Uterus

I can feel the baby kicking!

Goodness from the mother's food is carried along the cord to the baby

Egg cell divides again and again

Day 1

Day 2

Days 3–4

12 weeks
5 centimetres

20 weeks
16 centimetres

How fast does a baby grow?

Inside its mum, a baby grows really fast. It starts off as a tiny egg, which divides to make the billions of cells that make up the whole baby. After nine months, the baby is big enough to be born.

Protective fluid surrounds babies in the uterus

Can there be more than one baby?

If two eggs grow, or if one egg splits in half, there can be two babies — twins. Twins from two eggs look different, but twins from the same egg are identical.

WAAAH! WAAH!

32 weeks
42 centimetres

40 weeks
51 centimetres

Why do babies cry?

When babies are born, they can't talk or do anything for themselves. They cry to tell their parents that they're hungry, or they're cold — or that their nappy needs changing!

Am I always growing?

You keep growing from when you are born until your late teens or early twenties. But the speed you grow at slows down. A baby triples its weight in a year.

Do you know how tall you are?

Babies double their weight in five months. If you kept doing that you'd be huge!

5 years

6 months

Newborn

10 years

How do I get taller?

A soft, flexible substance called cartilage grows inside your bones, making them longer. The cartilage slowly hardens into bone.

Cartilage hardens to bone

Why does my hair need cutting?

Your hair grows throughout your life, so you have to keep cutting it. Hair grows from a little pit on your scalp called a hair follicle, but the hair you can see is actually dead. That's why it doesn't hurt to have a haircut.

Hair follicle

15 years

20 years

70 years

Your ears keep getting bigger too, but very slowly.

Grandma? Grandpa?

Do we shrink as we get older?

Yes! The bones of the spine get squashed closer together over the years. Some older people also get a curved spine and stoop, and that makes them look even shorter.

A compendium of questions

Why do my first teeth fall out?

Your first teeth are temporary – you have them until your mouth grows large enough for your permanent teeth. You have 20 first teeth, and they are replaced by larger, stronger, teeth.

What are hiccups?

If the muscle across your chest suddenly squeezes, it can snap shut the opening to your vocal flaps, making the 'hic' sound.

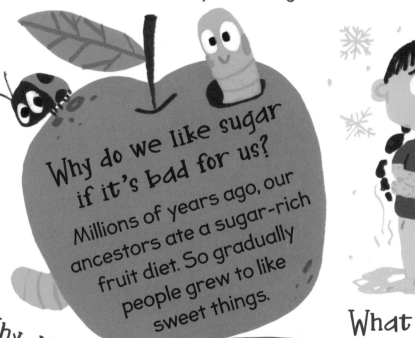

Why do we like sugar if it's bad for us?

Millions of years ago, our ancestors ate a sugar-rich fruit diet. So gradually people grew to like sweet things.

Why do i yawn?

No one's quite sure, but possibly as a way of getting more oxygen into your body quickly.

What are goosebumps?

They are bumps on your skin where tiny muscles make your hairs stand up if you are cold or scared.

Why do we get wrinkles?

As skin ages, it loses its elasticity, so it can't spring back into shape after stretching (such as when you smile).

Why don't I have to remember to breathe?

Your brain deals with all kinds of automatic activities without you having to think about them, including breathing, and digesting food.

What is my tummy button for?

When you were inside your mother, you got nutrients and oxygen through the umbilical cord that connected you to her body. The tummy button is what's left after the cord is cut.

Why is blood red?

Blood contains a chemical for carrying oxygen that contains iron. When this chemical picks up oxygen, it turns redder.

What makes a scab?

When your blood meets the air, special cells called platelets break up and mix with a protein in blood to make tangly fibres, forming a scab.

Why do I sleep more when I'm ill?

Your body needs energy to fight the illness, so to save energy it makes you sleep.

CURIOUS
questions &
answers about...
My Body

You're curious too, so we want to find out about YOU!

What's your NAME?

How OLD are you?

What colour are your eyes?

First published in 2019 by Miles Kelly Publishing Ltd
Harding's Barn, Bardfield End Green, Thaxted, Essex, CM6 3PX, UK

Copyright © Miles Kelly Publishing Ltd 2021

4 6 8 10 9 7 5 3

This edition printed 2021

Publishing Director Belinda Gallagher
Creative Director Jo Cowan
Editorial Director Rosie Neave
Design Manager Joe Jones
Image Manager Liberty Newton
Production Jennifer Brunwin
Reprographics Stephan Davis
Assets Lorraine King
Consultant Dr Kristina Routh

ISBN 978-1-78989-046-4

Printed in China

British Library Cataloguing-in-Publication Data
A catalogue record for this book is available from the British Library

Made with paper from a sustainable forest

www.mileskelly.net